# Diamonds

## For

# Mothers

## Words For Winning At Motherhood

# J. KONRAD HÖLÈ

Proverbs 4:7 says, "Wisdom is the Principle thing." Wisdom is the only proof that you are being **"Mentored"** by the **"Most Intelligent Person In The Universe,"** the "Holy Spirit."

Unless otherwise indicated, all Scripture quotations are taken from the King James Version of the Bible.

*Diamonds for Mothers*

Copyright © 1996 by J. Konrad Hölè
ISBN 1-888696-05-2
World Centre Ministries
P.O. Box 41010
Minneapolis, MN 55441

Published by
The World Press
P.O. Box 41010
Minneapolis, MN 55441

# Foreword

I realized that the closer I became to the **"Holy Spirit,"** who is the **"Spirit of Wisdom,"** not only would He teach me everything He knows, but He would ignite a craving within me to know more. You will never remember someone's **"Words,"** as much as you will remember someone's **"Point."** That is why I wrote this book. It is simply because I believe that one **"Diamond Key"** of wisdom can unlock a **"Vaulted Treasure"** of information.

You and I are only ever **"One Truth"** away from what we do not understand, and what we need to know. These are not copies of someone else's quotes, or revelation. These are **"Diamonds of Revelation"** that the "**Holy Spirit**" has unlocked to me in Crusades, Seminars, and Teachings around the world. Feel free to share these with someone that needs to know what you know.

**Diamonds** are not just a **"Girl's Bestfriend,"** they're everybody's **"BESTFRIEND."**

Enjoy.

J. Konrad

# Dedication

In my opinion a Faithful Mother is more important than even the President of the United States. This book is dedicated to three Queens that have best exemplified the special calling of Motherhood

My mother Joan, the person who paid for me to be where I am today in many ways, and believed in me when even some closest to me did not, I love you more than I can say! I'm definitely a "Mama's Boy."

My Grandmother Frances Bradway, A lady of the *Holy Spirit* who mentored me in the understanding of who He really was, and what He could be through my life if I would just stay faithful. If I could wish for anything, I would wish that you were still here.

My Grandmother Hölè, a woman of Integrity and Loyalty to the work of *God*, and a woman who's example of dedication to *God* and my Grandfather, will never be forgotten.

I love you all,

J. Konrad Hölé

# Table of Contents

| | |
|---|---|
| Achieving . . . . . . . . . 1 | Motivation . . . . . . . . .17 |
| Anger . . . . . . . . . . . .2 | Organization . . . . . . .18 |
| Assignment . . . . . . .3 | Pain . . . . . . . . . . . . .19 |
| Blessing . . . . . . . . . .4 | Patience . . . . . . . . . .20 |
| Change . . . . . . . . . . .5 | Pleasure . . . . . . . . . .21 |
| Communication . . . . .6 | Problem-Solving . . . .22 |
| Criticism . . . . . . . . .7 | Reactions . . . . . . . . .23 |
| Depression . . . . . . . .8 | Relationships . . . . . .24 |
| Excellence . . . . . . . .9 | Resources . . . . . . . . .25 |
| Fears . . . . . . . . . . . .10 | Schedule . . . . . . . . .26 |
| Forgiveness . . . . . . .11 | Strength . . . . . . . . . .27 |
| Health . . . . . . . . . . .12 | Stress . . . . . . . . . . . .28 |
| Hospitality . . . . . . . .13 | Thanksgiving . . . . . .29 |
| Instruction . . . . . . . .14 | Tragedy . . . . . . . . . .30 |
| Leadership . . . . . . . .15 | Understanding . . . . .31 |
| Mentorship . . . . . . .16 | Warfare . . . . . . . . . .32 |

# Achieving

**❶ Achievers** think silently, before they speak loudly.

**❷ Achievers** plan carefully, before they build largely.

**❸ Achievers** examine practically, before they react wisely.

**❹ Achievers** pursue intently, before they decide directionally.

**❺ Achievers** interrogate deeply, before they commit relationally.

**❻ Achievers** observe privately, before they react publicly.

**❼ Achievers** test indefinitely, before they trust loyally.

---
D i a m o n d    W o r d s

*The soul of the sluggard desireth, and hath nothing: but the soul of the diligent shall be made fat. Proverbs 13:4*

# Anger

**1** You will never change anything you don't hate.

**2** Your **Anger** is a link to the problems, *God* has called you to solve.

**3** Release your **Anger** when it's a "Puff," not an "Explosion."

**4** Be a "Victor," not a "Victim."

**5** **Anger** is the revealer of fear.

**6** Uncontrolled **Anger**, is the proof of unresolved hurt.

**7** Have enough fortitude to pick a side, and enough conviction to walk on it.

—— D i a m o n d   W o r d s ——
*Be not hasty in thy spirit to be angry: for **Anger** resteth in the bosom of fools.  Ecclesiastes 7:9*

# Assignment

**1** Your **Assignment** is proof *God* planned for you to succeed in something.

**2** When you're out of your **Assignment**, deception becomes rational, and error becomes probable.

**3** If *God* could have found a replacement for your **Assignment**, *He* would have never given it to you.

**4** Your **Assignment** is proof *God* preserved you, in order to preserve *His* purpose in you.

**5** Your **Assignment** will either be promoted, or distracted by a person.

**6** Never defend your **Assignment** to someone with a different one.

**7** If your life is not over, then neither is your **Assignment.**

---

### Diamond Words

*...the law is not made for a righteous man, but for the lawless and disobedient, for the ungodly and for sinners... I Timothy 1:9*

# Blessing

❶ A **Blessing** life will require a **Blessing** mentality.

❷ **Blessings** will often come from unpredictable sources, in unexplainable packages.

❸ **Blessings** will require you to look past the obvious, and see into the supernatural.

❹ **Blessings** are the proof of obedience.

❺ You must be as ruthless in protecting your **Blessings**, as you are in pursuing them.

❻ **Blessings** are motivated by Covenant Promise, not natural circumstance.

❼ **Blessings** can be scheduled into your life as easily as curses can.

―――――― D i a m o n d    W o r d s ――――――

*And all these **Blessings** shall come on thee, and overtake thee, if thou shalt hearken unto the voice of the LORD thy God   Deuteronomy 28:2*

# Change

**❶** Great leaders are quick to recognize error, and quicker to **Change** it.

**❷** *God* will always **Change** you to greater, never average.

**❸** *God* does not **Change** you to make you miserable, but to make you effective.

**❹** In order to get to where you want to be, you must be willing to leave where you are at.

**❺** *God* uses **Change** to clear your present canvas, so *He* can paint a future portrait.

**❻** **Change** what you believe, in order to **Change** what you achieve.  **Change** the way you talk, in order to **Change** the steps you walk.  **Change** the seed you sow, in order to **Change** the harvest you grow.

**❼** You will not succeed in your future, how you are in your present, so *God* makes **Changes** along the way.

---

### Diamond Words

*Being confident of this very thing, that he which hath begun a good work in you will perform it until the day of Jesus Christ   Philippians 1:6*

# Communication

**1** Your words will either build a platform to stand on, or dig a ditch to fall in.

**2** Speak from your passion, not from someone else's.

**3** Words are the only opportunity you have to enter someone's moment, and change their lifetime.

**4** Say in a sentence, what others say in a paragraph.

**5** If you cannot arrive at the point, don't go on the journey.

**6** Allow your mind to load the gun, before you allow your mouth to pull the trigger.

**7** **Communication** is the ability to take people on a journey from where they are, to where they need to be.

---
### Diamond Words

*Let no corrupt **Communication** proceed out of your mouth, but that which is good to the use of edifying   Ephesians 4:29*

# Criticism

**❶ Criticism** is just anothers way of envying your progress, and despising your difference.

**❷** Often times when others **Criticize** you it's because they see in you the boldness to be a "stone," instead of the fear in themselves to just be a piece of the rock.

**❸** Never defend your creativity to someone who is **Critical**.

**❹ Criticism** is a reaction of those who are intimidated in being "out done," more than motivated towards getting "more done."

**❺** Champions strategize, losers **Criticize**.

**❻** Those not making suggestions for your improvement, are unqualified to **Criticize** your achievements.

**❼ Criticism** will never destroy you, if it's not allowed to control you.

_____ D i a m o n d    W o r d s _____

*Having a good conscience; that, whereas they speak evil of you, as of evildoers, they may be ashamed that falsely accuse... I Peter 3:16*

# Depression

**1** The moment you stop moving toward something, **Depression** will make you a prisoner of nothing.

**2** **Depression** is the proof you have no photograph of a future.

**3** **Depression** is the devil's way of getting you one step closer to extinction.

**4** When vision walks out, **Depression** walks in.

**5** Misery is proof that what you're presently doing, is incapable of making you consistently happy.

**6** **Depression** is your enemies way of robbing your energy, by robbing your joy.

**7** You will only get **Depressed** at what you have, if you cannot see what *God* can do with it.

---

### Diamond Words

*Why art thou cast down, O my soul? and why art thou disquieted within me? hope thou in God: for I shall yet praise him, who is the health of my countenance, and my God   Psalms 42:11*

8

# Excellence

**❶ Excellence** will cost you what mediocrity will save you.

**❷ Excellent** people will conquer, what average people will complain about.

**❸ Excellent** people pursue solutions, average people stare at problems.

**❹ Excellence** orchestrates in your mind, translates in your speech, and demonstrates in your life.

**❺** Others will notice your effort to be **Excellent**, more than your acceptance to be mediocre.

**❻** Never expect someone else to tolerate the same lack of **Excellence,** that you would not.

**❼** Make improvements, not excuses.

---
Diamond Words

*In all things showing thyself a pattern of good works: in doctrine showing uncorruptness, gravity, sincerity   Titus 2:7*

---

# Fears

**1** Your assignment will reveal your **Fears**.

**2** The only walls that stop you, will be the ones you build yourself.

**3** You will never understand a person, until you understand a person's **Fears**.

**4** **Fears** must be understood, before they can be overcome.

**5** The more afraid you are to be yourself, the less afraid you'll be of being someone else.

**6** If you never **Fear** what is on the other side of right, you will never maintain a fortress against what is wrong.

**7** **FEAR**. False Evidence Appearing Real.

---

**—— D i a m o n d   W o r d s ——**

*For God hath not given us the spirit of fear; but of power, and of love, and of a sound mind. II Timothy 1:7*

# Forgiveness

**1** It's not temporary offenses that kill you, but rather your permanent attachment to them that does.

**2** What you cannot release, you cannot restore.

**3** **Forgiveness** does not stop someone else from causing pain, it stops you from having to live with it.

**4** *God* **Forgives** you, so you can **Forgive** yourself.

**5** You cannot change what is in another person, you can only change what is in you.

**6** *God* does not measure **Forgiveness** according to the severity of your sin, but according to the transparency of your heart.

**7** **Forgiveness** begins with your ability to live honest, not your ability to live perfect.

---
Diamond Words

*And be ye kind one to another, tenderhearted, **Forgiving** one another, even as God for Christ's sake hath **Forgiven** you   Ephesians 4:32*

# Health

◆ If **Health** does not matter to you, then healing is not your answer.

◆ A person that pursues **Health**, is a person who truly values what *God* has blessed them with.

◆ Healing is not a substitute for **Health**.

◆ How you protect *God's* blessing of "YOU," will determine how you will protect every other blessing *He* gives you.

◆ **Health** cannot be imparted, it must be pursued.

◆ Breakdown occurs when we attempt to get more out of our bodies, than we put in.

◆ **Health** decorates your appearance, and determines your endurance.

---
D i a m o n d    W o r d s

*Beloved, I wish above all things that thou mayest prosper and be in **Health**, even as thy soul prospereth   III John 1:2*

---

# Hospitality

**❶ Hospitality** is a seed *God* allows you to sow, to permit others to sow it into you.

**❷ Hospitality** disarms hostility.

**❸** Blessings are the proof, *God* has made it possible for you to be good to somebody.

**❹** Those who serve, are remembered as much as those who lead.

**❺** Excellence is impossible without **Hospitality**.

**❻ Hospitality** is proof you despise greed.

**❼ Hospitality** says anothers comfort matters to you as much as your own.

---

### Diamond Words

*That they do good, that they be rich in good works, ready to distribute, willing to communicate   I Timothy 6:18*

# Instruction

**1** If you cannot obey an **Instruction**, having a destination won't help you.

**2** You will always get more **Instructions**, before you get more blessings.

**3** Every time the *Holy Spirit* gives you an **Instruction**, *He* has already walked to the other side of it, and seen the eventuality of your obedience.

**4** The bridge between where you are, and where you want to be, will be built by acts of obedience.

**5** The *Holy Spirit* will never give you an **Instruction** to consider, *He* will give you an **Instruction** to follow.

**6** You are never qualified for a new **Instruction**, until you have obeyed a present one.

**7** Every time you ignore an **Instruction**, you abort a miracle.

---
### D i a m o n d     W o r d s

*...if thou shalt hearken diligently unto the voice of the LORD thy God, to observe and to do all his commandments... Deuteronomy 28:1*

---

# Leadership

**1** **Leadership** is the ability to lead somebody where you have been, rather than order them to go somewhere you have not.

**2** **Leaders** build memorials rather than create casualties.

**3** **Leadership** is the ability to motivate others to follow you, instead of force them to come.

**4** **Leaders** prepare others for their future, rather than possess others in their present.

**5** **Leaders** are former followers who mastered focus and conquered pride.

**6** **Leadership** is the ability to motivate everybody to do something, instead of somebody to do everything.

**7** **Leaders** learn from mistakes, followers live with them.

─────── D i a m o n d    W o r d s ───────

*And the things that thou hast heard of me among many witnesses, the same commit thou to faithful men, who shall be able to teach others also  II Timothy 2:2*

# Mentorship

**1** A **Mentor** is *God's* guarantee that your future will not be the same as your past.

**2** You do not decide who you will connect to, you discover whom *God* is linking you to.

**3** If somebody does not change from being in your life, then that is proof they did not come into your life to change.

**4** The rewards of your achievements will be accompanied by the responsibility to teach others to achieve.

**5** Proof of the kind of future *God* has assigned for you is determined by the kind of **Mentor** *He* connects you to.

**6** A **Mentor** already knows what he/she can do for the protégé, but it's not until the protege realizes what the **Mentor** can do, that the benefits of connection begin.

**7** A **Mentor** is proof that *God* thought enough of your assignment, that *He* gave you someone to help you achieve it.

───── D i a m o n d     W o r d s ─────

*And Joshua the son of Nun was full of the spirit of wisdom; for Moses had laid his hands upon him...Deuteronomy 34:9*

# Motivation

◆1 Improvements are only as quick, as your **Motivation** to correct deficiency.

◆2 Inferiority that is **Motivated**, will go further than superiority that is complacent.

◆3 Complacency never starts "big." It begins "small" and gains momentum.

◆4 The brick wall is not a sign your enemy has stopped you, it is a sign you have not found the door yet.

◆5 **Motivation** is what destroys complacency, and determines tenacity.

◆6 You will never be **Motivated** by anothers vision, unless it's your vision.

◆7 Move towards those who "energize where you are going," more than "sympathize with where you have come from."

———— D i a m o n d    W o r d s ————

*Be strong and of a good courage...for the LORD thy God, he it is that doth go with thee; he will not fail thee, nor forsake thee  Deuteronomy 31:6*

# Organization

**1** The longer you live with disorder, the longer you will live with the pain it produces.

**2** When something is in the right place, it can produce the right results.

**3** **Organization** will never begin, until the pain of clutter becomes too overwhelming.

**4** **Organize** your structure around what works best for who you are, and where you are at.

**5** If people don't know their position, they will never know their purpose.

**6** **Organize** your goals with an ending, not just a beginning.

**7** The first step towards **Organization**, is the honesty to admit  something is out of place.

---

D i a m o n d     W o r d s

*For God is not the author of confusion, but of peace, as in all churches of the saints*
*I Corinthians 14:33*

# Pain

**1** **Pain** is the motivator for change, that pleasure will never be.

**2** Expose Hurt.  Maintaining it makes it grow, releasing it makes it die.

**3** When you rehearse past mistakes, you prepare yourself to repeat them.

**4** You must agree to leave your past, before *God* can agree to start your future.

**5** **Pain** is only present when it is protected.

**6** You must interrogate the reasons why something has hurt you, before you can calculate a proper response to it.

**7** If **Pain** was never real, the ability to help others through it would not be possible.

---

Diamond   Words

*He healeth the broken in heart, and bindeth up their wounds   Psalms 147:3*

# Patience

**1** The purpose of the *Holy Spirit's* leading, is to birth the "conviction of **Patience**" in you, so your enemy will be unable to use the "weapon of **Impatience**" to sabotage your destiny.

**2** **Impatience** will rob time of being your ally.

**3** The only way *God's* purpose can come to pass, is if *God's* timing brings it.

**4** Most equate **Patience** with passivity. *God* equates it with trust.

**5** **Patience** will offend those not allowed to manipulate you with haste.

**6** **Patience** will keep you out of the "pit" of presumption.

**7** **Patience** disarms your enemies' strategy to abort the entry of something *God* has already scheduled into your future.

---
**————— D i a m o n d   W o r d s —————**

*But let **Patience** have her perfect work, that ye may be perfect and entire, wanting nothing*
*James 1:4*

# Pleasure

**1** **Pleasure** will never be present until it is scheduled.

**2** **Pleasure** is the ability to enjoy something you love.

**3** **Pleasure** will never be plentiful, until it is pursued.

**4** Schedule enough **Pleasure**, that regret has no room for accusation.

**5** Be good to yourself. How good you are to you, determines how good you are to others.

**6** Learn to disconnect. You can't clear your problems, until you can clear your mind.

**7** Make appointments to play, just like you make them to work.

---
D i a m o n d    W o r d s

*...Let the LORD be magnified, which hath*
***Pleasure** in the prosperity of his servant*
*Psalms 35:27*

# Problem–Solving

**1** Never complain about anything you won't attempt to solve.

**2** Average people point out problems, excellent people solve them.

**3** Those that never get involved, never get promoted.

**4** Those who do not solve problems, start them.

**5** **Problem–Solving** is determined by the willingness to react, more than the carelessness to observe.

**6** Problems you are incapable of solving, will not stand out to you.

**7** Diplomacy is the harbor through the storms of commitment.

---

——— D i a m o n d   W o r d s ———

*Without counsel purposes are disappointed: but in the multitude of counsellors they are established   Proverbs 15:22*

# Reactions

❶ Great leaders never answer something that has not been asked.

❷ The "High Road" will require as much humility, as integrity.

❸ One right **Reaction**, can position you for a lot of right favor.

❹ Wrong does not require two people.

❺ Anothers leverage against you, is based on how they think you will react.

❻ Don't analyze what you don't see, don't criticize what you don't understand.

❼ Right **Reactions** are the proof you have learned from the wrong ones.

───── D i a m o n d    W o r d s ─────

*He that answereth a matter before he heareth it, it is folly and shame unto him. Proverbs 18:13*

# Relationship

**1** When *God* wants to birth a future, *He* births a **Relationship**. When the enemy wants to destroy a future, he births a **Relationship**.

**2** Unnecessary **Relationships** produce unrealistic expectations.

**3** Opposition is never present until multiplication is possible.

**4** You will be known as much for the people you avoid, as much as the ones you associate with.

**5** Never attempt to take people past the "expiration date" of their seasons in your life.

**6** Celebrate the "Seasons" *God* puts people in your life, and the "Reasons" *He* takes them out.

**7** Don't be a "pack rat" of wrong people.

---
**D i a m o n d    W o r d s**

*Be ye not unequally yoked together with unbelievers: for what fellowship hath righteousness with unrighteousness?... II Corinthians 6:14*

---

# Resources

◆1 You will never reach for the expertise of others, until you acknowledge your own weakness.

◆2 The sacrifice of something you want, will determine the possession of something you want more.

◆3 Never ask directions, from someone who does not understand where you are going.

◆4 The life long "School of Wisdom" has varied teachers.  Dip your pail in the wells of many.

◆5 Those you become linked to, are those you will imitate.

◆6 The moment you invite corrupt individuals into your assignment, is the moment you invite their tragedy to sabotage it.

◆7 If you could succeed alone, you would have already reached the top!

—————— D i a m o n d   W o r d s ——————

*Go to the ant, thou sluggard; consider her ways, and be wise:  Which having no guide, overseer, or ruler, Provideth her meat in the summer, and gathereth her food in the harvest.  Proverbs 6:6-8*

# Schedule

**1** If you don't plan your **Schedule**, you will be dominated by someone else's.

**2** Those that will distract your **Schedule**, are those that do not have one themselves.

**3** **Schedule** something daily that you love to do, as much as you **Schedule** something daily that you have to do.

**4** If you do not value time, you will never value your assignment.

**5** Unless you value your own **Schedule**, you will never be considerate of someone else's.

**6** **Schedule** the exit of something, at the same time you **Schedule** the entrance.

**7** When you document your day, you determine the strategies for tomorrow.

---

**D i a m o n d   W o r d s**

*Redeeming the time, because the days are evil*
*Ephesians 5:16*

---

# Strength

**1** **Strength** is determined by focus. What you look at either motivates you, or stagnates you.

**2** Never use the **Strength** for achieving your goal, convincing others to believe in it.

**3** Disconnect from those who "sympathize" where you are at, and move towards those who "energize" where you are going.

**4** You will use more **Strength** pursuing an option, than you will following an instruction.

**5** What you have a "love for," you will have a "longevity in."

**6** **Strength** must be "daily renewed," or it will be "eventually expired."

**7** The strategy to replace a mistake, comes from the honesty to admit you made one.

---

### D i a m o n d    W o r d s

*But they that wait upon the LORD shall renew their **Strength**; they shall mount up with wings as eagles; they shall run, and not be weary; and they shall walk, and not faint   Isaiah 40:31*

# Stress

**1** **Stress** magnifies when you're not in the "Center of your Expertise."

**2** Disobedience produces need.

**3** **Stressful** decisions produce **Stressful** conditions.

**4** Unrealistic focus, produces unnecessary **Stress**.

**5** **Stress** never changes, until your tolerance level for it does.

**6** **Stress** is not the presence of adversity, it's the absence of direction.

**7** For every day you're not soaring in the "Secret Place," you're surviving in the "**Stress** Place."

---

— D i a m o n d    W o r d s —
*Better is a dry morsel, and quietness therewith, than an house full of sacrifices with strife.*
*Proverbs 17:1*

# Thanksgiving

**1** Gratitude expands your boundaries for blessing.

**2** Gratitude releases others to be generous to you.

**3** Reward those who helped you, that did not have to.

**4** Go the extra mile to reward those that went the extra mile.

**5** **"Thank You"** is the ageless term, with "Endless Rewards."

**6** When you're **Thankful**, you're teachable.

**7** People are touched by gratitude, more than they are impressed with aptitude.

---

D i a m o n d    W o r d s

*Let us come before his presence with **Thanksgiving**, and make a joyful noise unto him with psalms   Psalms 95:2*

# Tragedy

**1** If you wait to release a **Tragedy** until you can explain it, you will place your recovery on indefinite delay.

**2** If you never get over the reasons of why you fell down, you will never grasp the reasons for why you should get back up.

**3** Champions move beyond, where losers choose to stay.

**4** Those that can survive a crash, are greater than those that think they never will.

**5** *God* can enter through the "trap door" of a mistake, and lead you to the place *He* was unable to lead you prior to that point.

**6** If your desire does not move you towards *God,* your calamity will.

**7** When you have nothing left but *God,* you have got enough to start again (Mike Murdock).

---
### Diamond Words

*...Give unto them beauty for ashes, the oil of joy for mourning, the garment of praise for the spirit of heaviness... Isaiah 61:3*

---

# Understanding

**1** **Understanding** is the tool the *Holy Spirit* uses to process "wisdom."

**2** You cannot **Understand** anothers position, until you can **Understand** anothers pain.

**3** Give others enough space to turn around, the same amount that you would need.

**4** Excellent people observe, average people react.

**5** You cannot **Understand** another's fears, until you can **Understand** another's failures.

**6** You will never **Understand** who you are, until you **Understand** why you are here.

**7** You will never **Understand** the power of "short term decisions," until you put everything through the "long range process."

---
Diamond   Words

*Wisdom is the principal thing; therefore get wisdom: and with all thy getting get* ***Understanding*** *Proverbs 4:7*

# Warfare

**1** The object of **Warfare**, is to get someone bigger than your enemy to stand up on your battlefield.

**2** The purpose of **Warfare** is to reap the bounty, not magnify the battle.

**3** Every battle that *God* is not allowed to fight, you will have to.

**4** **Warfare** begins with movement.

**5** Never give opposition an explanation.

**6** **Warfare** is the prelude to promotion.

**7** When you maximize the size of your *God*, you minimize the size of your enemy.

---

**D i a m o n d    W o r d s**

*For in the time of trouble he shall hide me in his pavilion: in the secret of his tabernacle shall he hide me; he shall set me up upon a rock   Psalms 27:5*

# Signs & Wonders Partners

I want ot take this time and personally say how *"Excited"* and *"Grateful"* I am to God for the many friends from all parts of these United States that have become linked to this *Ministry of the Holy Spirit* with their prayers and with their monthly seed into this fertile soil of this harvest field. Having the privilege of the taking the message of this *"Wonderful Companion"* to thousands around the country in both live crusades and media outreach, has been a joy that words cannot express.

I know there are still yet many of you that *God's voice* is going to speak to, to become connected with this ministry as a special *"Signs and Wonders Partner"* both prayerfully and financially to help take this message of knowing the *Holy Spirit* to so many that still need to hear it.

Would you ask the *Holy Spirit* today about becoming linked with me at *$10.00 each month*, or whatever *He* lays upon your heart so we can reach this critical objective together. Remember, *whenever you react to His voice, He reacts to your future*.

I'll look forward to hearing from you.

☐ **Yes, J. Konrad I want to link myself to you with my monthly seed of $_____ a month for the spreading of this needed message around the world!**

Name _____

Address _____

City _____State _____Zip _____

Phone ( )_____

**Clip & Mail To: Spirit & Life Ministries**
**P.O. BOX 41010  MINNEAPOLIS, MN 55441**

# Let Me Agree With You In Prayer For Your Need!

You are daily upon my heart and your needs matter greatly to me. Don't ever think that you are alone. I want to agree with you that the Holy Spirit will bring the provision of God in your life!

Clip & Mail

Name _____

Address _____

City _____State _____Zip _____

Phone ( )_____

**Clip & Mail To: Spirit & Life Ministries**
**P.O. BOX 41010   MINNEAPOLIS, MN 55441**

# More Power-Packed Teaching
# From J. Konrad Hölè

### The Leading Of His Spirit

Join J. Konrad for this "Explosive" and "In-Depth" study on how the Holy Spirit leads you more by "Purpose, Principals and Protocal" than He does by Euphoria, Emotion, and Excitement. The greatest seasons of your life are just ahead, LED BY HIS SPIRIT.

**$20.00 (4 tape series)**

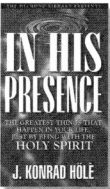

### In His Presence

Find out the life changing secrets of Kind David's revelation of how to live in the Presence of God. The most incredible breakthroughs in your life are about to take place just be being in His Presence.

**$15.00 (3 tape series)**

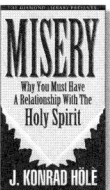

### Diary Of The Holy Spirit

Discover the benefits of how to Commune, Flow, Discern, and Listen to the Holy Spirit who Jesus said would be with you Always. Your greatest relationship is one revelation away.

**$15.00 (3 tape series)**

### Misery

Discover David's revelation principles from Psalms 16:11, that the only true place of joy was in God's presence, and that anything outside His presence was not designed to satisfy you, but rather would be a source of "Misery."

**$20.00 (4 tape series)**

### The Mentor And The Protege

What is a *Mentor*? A gift by *God* to insure the success of completing your *Assignment*. What is a *Protege*? A person whose future depends on the impartation from somebody who has already been where they are going. In this impactive teaching you will understand the purpose of mentoring.

**$20.00 (4 tape series)**

# "The Diamond Library For Achievers"
## Several Dynamic Topics:

## Build Your Complete Achiever Library!

### Obedience

Join J. Konrad for this "Impactive" study on the "Power" of OBEDIENCE and its ability to be the bridge from "Where You Are," to "Where You Want To Be ," and God's ability to react to your life everytime you follow one of "His Instructions."
**$10.00 (2 tapes)**

### Time

Join J. Konrad for this "Impactive" study on the "Currency of TIME," its ability to form your "Destiny" around you, and its critical role in developing your relationship with the Holy Spirit.
**$10.00 (2 tapes)**

### Focus

Join J. Konrad for this "Impactive" study on the Force of "FOCUS," and its ability to enable you to walk through the "Valleys of Distraction," and complete your life assignment!
**$10.00 (2 tapes)**

## Send Your Order In Today!

### Seed-Faith

Join J. Konrad for this "Impactive" study on the "Power Of Seed Movement" in your life, and your ability to take something God has placed in your hand, to create something God has ordained in your life.
**$10.00 (2 tapes)**

### Warfare

Join J. Konrad for this "Impactive" study of how you were not called to be a "Captive," you were called to be a "Deliverer."
**$10.00 (2 tapes)**

### Direction

Join J. Konrad for this "Impactive" study on how the "HOLY SPIRIT" answers one of the most pivotal questions ever in your life... the question of DIRECTION.!
**$10.00 (2 tapes)**

**SPECIAL PACKAGE PRICE... Receive all 6 titles into your life for just $30. (please specify when ordering)**

*Don't let these opportunities pass you by! Rush your order in today. Fill out the form below. Please print clearly and legibly. Ask the Holy Spirit what Seed He would have you to sow into this world-changing ministry.*

| Title | Qty. | Price | Total |
|---|---|---|---|
| The Leading Of His Spirit (Tapes) | | $ | $ |
| In His Presence (Tapes) | | $ | $ |
| The Diary Of The Holy Spirit (Tapes) | | $ | $ |
| Misery (Tapes) | | $ | $ |
| The Mentor And The Protege (Tapes) | | $ | $ |
| Library For Achievers - Time (Tapes) | | $ | $ |
| Library For Achievers - Obedience (Tapes) | | $ | $ |
| Library For Achievers - Focus (Tapes) | | $ | $ |
| Library For Achievers - Seed-Faith (Tapes) | | $ | $ |
| Library For Achievers - Warfare (Tapes) | | $ | $ |
| Library For Achievers - Direction (Tapes) | | $ | $ |
| 1 Item......................$2 - S/H | Shipping/Handling | | $ |
| 2 Items...................$3 - S/H | Seed-Faith Gift | | $ |
| 3 or more Items.....$4 - S/H | Total | | $ |

☐ J. Konrad, please send me my **FREE** copy of your *Spirit & Life Talk* newsletter.

☐ Check    ☐ Money Order    ☐ Visa    ☐ MasterCard

Card No. ☐☐☐☐☐☐☐☐☐☐☐☐☐☐☐☐

Exp. Date _____ Signature _____

Name _____

Address _____

City _____ State _____ Zip _____

Phone ( )_____

**Clip & Mail To: Spirit & Life Ministries**
**P.O. BOX 41010   MINNEAPOLIS, MN 55441**

Clip & Mail

## Choose From These Exciting Titles! Books that will bring a Breakthrough... Your life will be challenged and changed with revelation knowledge!

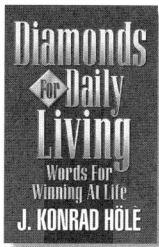

Clip & Mail

**Diamonds For Daily Living**

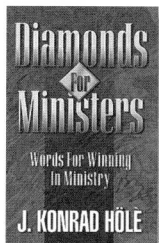

**Diamonds For Ministers**

**Diamonds For Mothers**

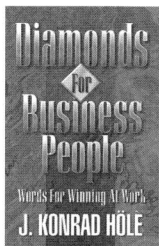

**Diamonds For Business People**

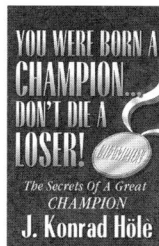

**You Were Born A Champion... Don't Die A Loser!**

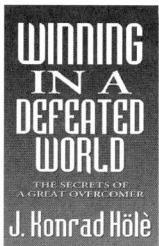

**Winning In A Defeated World**

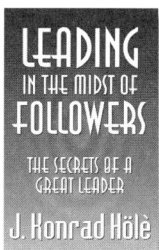

**Leading In the Midst Of Followers**

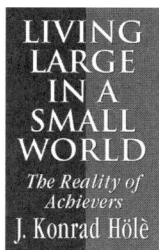

**Living Large In A Small World**

**See the next page for details on how to order your personal copies of these books!**

# "Literature Evangelism Team"

## Order Form

☐ Yes, J. Konrad, I want to be a part of this "Evangelism Breakthrough" so that I may affect those that God links me to with the power of revelation knowledge.

*Order a set of 10 copies of any title for $10. You may also mix titles of the books to bring a total of 10 copies for $10. Order for your friends and family!*

| Title | Qty. (Sets of 10) | Price | Total |
|---|---|---|---|
| Diamonds For Daily Living | | x $10 | $ |
| Diamonds For Ministers | | x $10 | $ |
| Diamonds For Mothers | | x $10 | $ |
| Diamonds For Business People | | x $10 | $ |
| You Were Born A Champion... | | x $10 | $ |
| Winning In A Defeated World | | x $10 | $ |
| Leading In The Midst Of Followers | | x $10 | $ |
| Living Large In A Small World | | x $10 | $ |
| Add $2 For Shipping | Shipping | | $ |
| | Seed-Faith Gift | | $ |
| | Total | | $ |

☐ Check ☐ Money Order ☐ Visa ☐ MasterCard

Card No. ☐☐☐☐☐☐☐☐☐☐☐☐☐☐☐☐

Exp. Date _____ Signature _____

Name _____

Address _____

City _____ State _____ Zip _____

Phone ( )_____

**Clip & Mail To: Spirit & Life Ministries**
**P.O. BOX 41010   MINNEAPOLIS, MN 55441**

Clip & Mail